SPOTLIGHT ON SPACE SCIENCE

JOURNEY THROUGH GALAXIES

LORI SMYER

PowerKiDS
press.

New York

Published in 2015 by The Rosen Publishing Group, Inc.
29 East 21st Street, New York, NY 10010

First Edition

Editor: Susan Meyer
Book Design: Kris Everson

Photo Credits: Cover (main) NASA/JPL-Caltech/University of Wisconsin; cover (galaxy icon) GSFC; p. 5 inigofotografia/iStock/Thinkstock; p. 7 NASA, ESA, STScI, J. Hester and P. Scowen (Arizona State University); p. 9 (spiral galaxy) NASA, ESA, the Hubble Heritage Team (STScI/AURA), and R. Gendler (for the Hubble Heritage Team); p. 9 (barred spiral) NASA, ESA, and the Hubble Heritage Team (STScI/AURA)-ESA/Hubble Collaboration; p. 9 (elliptical) NASA, ESA, and the Hubble Heritage Team (STScI/AURA); p. 11 NASA; p. 13 NASA/JPL-Caltech/R. Hurt (SSC); p. 15 (top) NASA/JPL-Caltech/UCLA; p. 15 (bottom) The Hubble Heritage Team (AURA/STScI/NASA); p.17 NASA, ESA, Digitized Sky Survey (DSS; STScI/AURA/UKSTU/AAO), H. Richer and J. Heyl (University of British Columbia), and J. Anderson and J. Kalirai (STScI); p. 19 NASA, ESA, and Z. Levay (STScI/AURA); p. 21 Andromeda: T. Rector and B. Wolpa (NOAO/AURA/NSF); p. 23 NASA, ESA, Z. Levay and R. van der Marel (STScI), T. Hallas, and A. Mellinger; p. 25 ESA, NASA and Robert A.E. Fosbury (European Space Agency/Space Telescope-European Coordinating Facility, Germany); p. 27 NASA, ESA, H. Teplitz and M. Rafelski (IPAC/Caltech), A. Koekemoer (STScI), R. Windhorst (Arizona State University), and Z. Levay (STScI); p. 29 (distant galaxy) NASA, ESA, M. Postman and D. Coe (STScI), and the CLASH Team; p. 29 (Hubble) NASA.

Library of Congress Cataloging-in-Publication Data

Smyer, Lori.
Journey through galaxies / by Lori Smyer.
p. cm. — (Spotlight on space science)
Includes index.
ISBN 978-1-4994-0369-5 (pbk.)
ISBN 978-1-4994-0398-5 (6-pack)
ISBN 978-1-4994-0414-2 (library binding)
1. Galaxies — Juvenile literature. I. Title.
QB857.3 S69 2015
523.1—d23
Manufactured in the United States of America

CPSIA Compliance Information: Batch #CW15PK: For Further Information contact Rosen Publishing, New York, New York at 1-800-237-9932

CONTENTS

MILLIONS AND BILLIONS OF STARS

CHAPTER 1

If Earth had a space address, it would be "Earth, The Solar System, The Milky Way, The Universe." So what is the Milky Way?

The Milky Way is a **galaxy**. It is a huge collection of **stars**, gas, and dust. Our whole solar system is just a tiny, tiny part of it. If that's hard to imagine, let's do the math.

In 1977, two National Aeronautics and Space Administration (NASA) spacecraft, *Voyager 1* and *Voyager 2,* left Earth. By 2011, *Voyager 1* and *Voyager 2* had made it to the outer regions of our solar system. Even though they were traveling at speeds of about 34,000 miles an hour (54,700 km/h), the two spacecraft still took over 30 years just to reach the edge of our solar system.

Now think about this. The distance across the Milky Way is the same as 50,000 solar systems laid end to end. When it comes to all things **galactic**, huge is seriously huge!

This photo shows the Milky Way from Earth, which is located inside the galaxy.

GALAXIES APLENTY!
CHAPTER 2

The Milky Way galaxy is so vast it's hard to imagine anything beyond it. The Milky Way is not alone in space, though. **Astronomers** estimate that there are over 100 billion galaxies in the universe!

Galaxies come in many different sizes. Astronomers believe that some giant galaxies may be home to one hundred trillion stars! Dwarf, or small, galaxies may have only around 10 million stars.

Galaxies are places where stars are born, live, and die—over millions and millions of years. Inside galaxies, stars are born in huge clouds of dust and gas known as **nebulae**. As a nebula begins to shrink under its own gravity, it breaks into clumps. These clumps become so hot and dense that they ignite and become stars.

Everything in a galaxy—nebulae, stars, planets, dust, and gas—is held together by gravity.

These vast columns of gas and dust in the Milky Way's Eagle Nebula are slowly condensing into stars.

ALL SHAPES AND SIZES

CHAPTER 3

Galaxies don't just come in different sizes. They can also be described by their shapes.

Spiral galaxies have a circular or disk shape. Arms made of stars branch out from the center of the galaxy. The arms form a shape similar to streams of water spiraling out from a rotating lawn sprinkler.

Barred spiral galaxies have a huge cloud of stars at their center shaped like a football. This star cloud is known as the bar. The galaxy's arms branch out from the ends of the bar.

Elliptical galaxies are vast collections of stars grouped in a round or oval shape. These galaxies look like massive starry soccer balls or footballs.

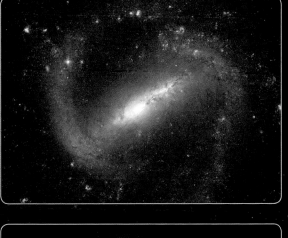

This barred spiral galaxy, NGC 1073, is a little smaller than the Milky Way.

This elliptical galaxy, M87, is home to trillions of stars.

9

MEASURING AT THE SPEED OF LIGHT

CHAPTER 4

When we travel on Earth, we measure the distance in miles or kilometers. We can do the same when measuring distances in our solar system. The Sun, for example, is about 93 million miles (149.7 million km) from Earth. When it comes to measuring beyond our solar system, however, the distances are too big to use miles or kilometers.

To measure the size of galaxies and other distances in space, scientists use a unit of measurement called a **light-year**. The fastest thing we know of is light. It travels at about 186,500 miles per second (300,000 km/s). A light-year is the distance that light can travel in one year.

So how long is one light-year? The answer to that question is about 5,880,000,000,000 miles (9,460,000,000,000 km), or more than 5.8 trillion miles (9.4 trillion km)!

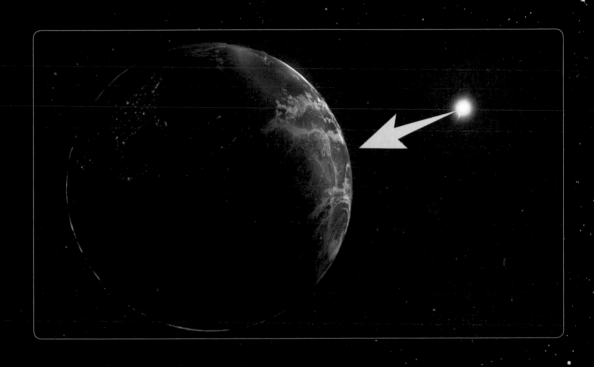

Light travels from the Sun to Earth in 8 minutes. A light-year is 63,421 times longer than the distance from the Sun to Earth.

OUR GALAXY

CHAPTER 5

Our Milky Way galaxy is home to between 200 and 400 billion stars. To cross it, you would have to travel a distance of about 100,000 light-years!

The Milky Way is a barred spiral galaxy. The central part of the galaxy is made up of a giant ball of millions of stars called the galactic bulge. Around the bulge, more stars, gas, and dust create a huge disk. The disk has a depth of around 1,000 light years! The galaxy's arms branch out from the disk.

At the center of the bulge is a **black hole**. Astronomers say that this black hole was formed by a massive star that died out and collapsed on itself. This created an incredibly compact, dense object. Its gravitational force is so powerful that nothing in its inner orbit, not even other stars or light itself, can escape being drawn into it!

This artwork shows the Milky Way from above. Our Sun is 26,000 light-years from the center of our galaxy.

CLUSTERS OF STARS
CHAPTER 6

The Milky Way contains many star clusters. A cluster is a group of stars that formed around the same time. Each star cluster is held together by gravity.

Open clusters are star clusters with no regular shape. They may contain thousands of stars, or as few as 12.

The Pleiades, or Seven Sisters, is an open star cluster 425 light-years from Earth. The cluster contains hundreds of stars, including a small number that can be seen at night without a telescope. The seven brightest stars give the cluster its alternative name of the Seven Sisters.

Globular clusters are balls of stars that are usually around 60 to 100 light-years in diameter. A globular cluster may contain as many as one million stars.

M80 is a globular cluster about 28,000 light-years from Earth. This cluster is home to hundreds of thousands of stars.

The Pleiades are surrounded by colorful interstellar dust.
We cannot see this dust from Earth.

There are about 150 globular clusters in the Milky Way.
M80 is one of the densest.

WHAT ELSE IS OUT THERE?

CHAPTER 7

All of the stars, planets, dust, and gas in the Milky Way make up only a small part of the total matter in our galaxy. So what makes up the other part? Right now, scientists don't know the answer to this question!

So how do they actually know something else is out there?

Scientists understand how gravity works. They can figure out how much gravity an object creates and how it affects other objects. Astronomers now know that the gravity created by visible matter is not strong enough to explain how fast our galaxy's stars are moving.

This means there is some other kind of matter out there creating gravity. Scientists have named it **dark matter**.

As yet, scientists do not know what dark matter is. A huge amount of our galaxy and universe is made of something completely new to us!

The 47 Tucanae globular cluster of stars is a breathtaking collection of "bright matter." It's the dark matter between and around the stars that is the new challenge for scientists to identify!

GALAXY GAZING

CHAPTER 8

Early astronomers and scientists were aware of the Milky Way long before telescopes were invented. In modern times, however, it has become harder to see the Milky Way with the naked eye. Lights from buildings and cars fill the night sky with a glow that blocks out the wonders of our home galaxy.

It is still possible, however, to view the Milky Way with just your eyes if the conditions are right. You will need to be in the countryside or in an isolated area, such as a desert. Viewing the Milky Way with the naked eye is best done in the summer or winter, on a night with no moonlight.

Seen from Earth with the naked eye, the Milky Way looks like a misty cloud dotted with stars.

As long as your location is dark enough, you can see the Milky Way from anywhere on Earth.

THE LOCALS

CHAPTER 9

The Milky Way belongs to a group of around 50 galaxies known as the "Local Group of Galaxies," or "Local Group." The Local Group is about 10 million light-years wide!

Just as Earth orbits the Sun, and the Sun orbits the center of the Milky Way, our galaxy and its neighbors are orbiting a central point in the Local Group, all held together by gravity.

The Local Group has two large spiral galaxies— the Milky Way and our nearest large neighbor, Andromeda. Other neighbors include a small spiral galaxy, the Triangulum Galaxy, and the Large Magellanic Cloud and the Small Magellanic Cloud. There are also a number of dwarf galaxies.

In galactic terms, "local" can be a long, long way. Andromeda is 2.6 million light-years away. When the light we see from Andromeda began its journey toward Earth, humans did not yet exist!

THE MILKY WAY'S NEIGHBOR

CHAPTER 10

The nearest galaxy similar in shape to our own Milky Way is the Andromeda Galaxy. Andromeda is also known as Messier 31. Information gathered by NASA's Spitzer Space Telescope suggests that this galaxy may contain around one trillion stars.

Andromeda is larger than the Milky Way with more stars. Scientists believe that the Milky Way has more mass, however, because of the amount of dark matter it contains.

The Andromeda Galaxy is on a collision course with the Milky Way. It is moving toward our galaxy at a speed of around 310,000 miles an hour (500,000 km/h). The two galaxies may eventually collide—in about five billion years! Astronomers believe that if this happens, the two galaxies will merge and form a giant elliptical galaxy.

What would the Andromeda-Milky Way collision look like? Over billions of year, the event would tear apart both galaxies before merging them. This is what it would look like from Earth.

SUPERBIG SUPERCLUSTERS

CHAPTER 11

Some groups of galaxies—such as the Local Group, which contains the Milky Way and Andromeda galaxies—are called clusters. However, some galactic groupings are even bigger than clusters. Clusters of clusters are called superclusters!

Some superclusters are made up of just a few galaxy groups. Others contain hundreds of groups. The Local Group belongs to a supercluster called the Virgo Supercluster. This supercluster contains at least 100 smaller galaxy clusters, including our Local Group.

Astronomers are finding that even superclusters are just small parts of much bigger galactic structures. A Great Wall is a massive group made up of many superclusters. In 2003, astronomers discovered the largest Great Wall yet. Situated about one billion light-years from

Earth, the Sloan Great Wall is a vast grouping of superclusters 1.5 billion light-years long!

This is a view of a supercluster called the Lynx Arc. It is one of the hottest, brightest, most active objects found in space. Scientists call it a "super star-birth region."

GALACTIC EXPLORATION
CHAPTER 12

From 2003 to 2004, the Hubble Space Telescope was used to examine one tiny area of space that contained no visible stars. What Hubble found was that this seemingly empty area is actually home to 10,000 galaxies.

Hubble focused two cameras on one point in space. The area surveyed was so small that astronomers described it as being like looking at a section of space through a soda straw. Over four months, Hubble took 800 pictures of this region. When combined, these pictures form an image known as the Hubble Ultra Deep Field.

The Ultra Deep Field image showed that in that one "soda-straw-sized" sliver of space, there are 10,000 galaxies. Hubble observed galaxies of different ages, shapes, and sizes. Some are "near" to our part of the universe, and some are very far away.

This 2014 version of the Ultra Deep Field image contains even more galaxies than the original. It includes celestial objects of every age, shape, size, and color.

GAZING ON THE PAST
CHAPTER 13

The Hubble Ultra Deep Field image will help astronomers find out more about galaxies. It will also help us find out more about the formation of our universe because it allows us to look back in time!

Some of the most distant galaxies in the Hubble Ultra Deep Field image are over 12 billion light-years away. Traveling at the fastest speed we know of, the light from stars in those galaxies began heading toward us billions of years before the Sun or our Earth came into being. In fact, the light has been heading toward Earth for nearly the entire lifetime of our universe. What we are seeing is how these galaxies looked in the very distant past.

Think of it like this: If we wanted to know what each of those distant galaxies looked like today, we would have to wait 12 billion years for the light to reach us!

Hubble is taking us back to the beginning. It has found some of the earliest galaxies. This one formed 420 million years after the start of the universe. Its light has traveled 13.3 billion years to reach Hubble.

OLD GALAXY

HUBBLE SPACE TELESCOPE

GLOSSARY

astronomer: A person who studies stars, planets, and other objects in outer space.

black hole: An invisible area in outer space with gravity so strong that light cannot get out of it.

dark matter: Matter that has no light and has not yet been directly detected by astronomers, but is believed to exist to account for various observed gravitational effects.

galactic: Of or relating to any one of the very large groups of stars that make up the universe.

galaxy: Any one of the very large groups of stars that make up the universe.

light-year: A unit of distance equal to the distance that light travels in one year, which is about 5.8 trillion miles (9.4 trillion km).

nebula: A cloud of gas and dust in outer space, visible in the night sky either as a bright patch or as a dark patch against other luminous matter.

star: Any one of the objects in space that are made of burning gas and that look like points of light in the night sky.

FOR MORE INFORMATION

BOOKS

Kopp, Megan. *The Milky Way and Other Galaxies.* Mankato, MN: Capstone Press, 2012.

Sabatino, Michael. *20 Fun Facts About Galaxies.* New York, NY: Gareth Stevens Publishing, 2015.

Thomas, Isabel. *Stars and Galaxies.* Chicago, IL: Raintree, 2013.

Trammel, Howard K. *Galaxies.* New York, NY: Children's Press, 2010.

WEBSITES

Due to the changing nature of Internet links, PowerKids Press has developed an online list of websites related to the subject of this book. This site is updated regularly. Please use this link to access the list: www.powerkidslinks.com/soss/gala

INDEX